Pearls From My *Tante*

Life Lessons You Won't Learn in the Classroom

Pearls From My Tante

Life Lessons You Won't Learn in the Classroom

Gayle LaSalle

Pearls From My Tante
Life Lessons You Won't Learn in the Classroom

ISBN: 978-0-557-06629-2

Sarah "Sekie" Rothkopf

My Tante

Dedication

The first dedication for this book is to my wonderful, insightful ***Tante Sekie***. Without her incredible wisdom and ability to share it with such sensitivity and humor, this book would not exist. However, there's more to my dedication to ***Tante Sekie***. Without this same wisdom and her willingness to share it, I wouldn't be who I am, nor have the passion I have to share with all who read this. Throughout my life, even when I didn't always realize it, My ***Tante Sekie*** was providing me with lessons. Her warmth, non-judgmental nature and acceptance were a solace for me in times when I most needed it. In recent years, I have learned to value her gentle advice and role modeling in ways that continue to challenge me and to spur me on to be the best person I'm capable of being. I owe ***My Tante*** more than I'll ever be able to express. I hope this book can demonstrate just a small part of how important a role she has played in my life.

Without a doubt, nothing I do in life would be the same without my daughter, Dania, who simply makes life worth living and whom I could not love more. She has been - for 28 years - and continues to be my inspiration and motivation for all things good. This inspiration and motivation has only become greater by the recent addition of our beautiful, beloved Kennedy -- my first and most wonderful granddaughter as well as her new sister McKenna – another granddaughter for me to love.

Acknowledgements

Contributions to this work include my cousin Laurie Sneider and both her daughters (Tante Sekie's granddaughters), Nicole Sneider Kaplan and Danielle Sneider Shaw. It was wonderful to hear how ***My Tante's*** wisdom impacted each of them. Hearing and sharing their stories has confirmed my belief that ***My Tante*** has touched so many more people, than just me. I admire my cousin Laurie for her friendship and for the wonderful daughters she raised. I admire her daughters, for the girls they were growing up, and for the women they have become, as the wives and mothers they are now.

I could not complete any project in my life without also thanking those other cheerleaders including all my friends, colleagues, and family members who encouraged me when I became frustrated or stalled. I have become grateful for all the "yay-sayers" in life – a term I learned from listening to Ann Tardy and her concept of Life Moxie (www.lifemoxie.com)

Particular thanks go to Natalie Sillary -of The Saratoga Trunk in Saratoga Springs, NY, and Janelle Pfister for their friendship and exceptional proofreading skills, which were generously donated to the cause.

To Julia Brannon, my friend and "sister" – there is no greater yay-sayer, in my life. And, to Patty Wilock who nourishes me in so many ways, that only a friend can.

My wonderful friend and exceptionally talented photographer, John Blackmer donated his time and energy for all the photos including the cover of this book. To him, a great big thank you and hug.

Last, but definitely, not least, a huge thank you to Dania, my darling daughter. She lived through the ups and downs with me. I so hope she has also benefited, and continues to benefit, from the lessons I've learned as well as some she may have picked up herself.

There are so many people who have encouraged me and cheered me on. I wish I could thank all on this page. You all know who you are and I say a great big – THANK YOU!

Contents

Forward

A Grand Daughter's Perspective of My Tante

By Danielle Sneider Shaw

My grandma is the most amazing being I know. She is filled with wisdom and love. She has the ability to touch the life of everyone who is fortunate enough to meet her.

I remember her talking of her time as an aide in a classroom with students having emotional and mental challenges. At times she encountered students who were filled with frustration and anger. One such student has written the f" word on his paper. She told the young man that she could turn the "f" word into a book. She then proceeded to change the F into a B, the u into an o, and the c into an o. At that moment, she had connected with a child who had previously shut himself out to others. She had gained his trust and could move forward and help him learn.

This story illustrates the type of person my grandma is. She is always finding a positive in situations. She has the ability to touch lives with the power of the love she emanates from her heart and the wisdom she pours out from her soul. She has an amazing ability to connect with others. She even was able to connect with and teach her dog how to say words like, Alvin and Havah Nigilah!

My grandma has always been there for me, to help me, guide me, and support me. Even as a child, when I made mistakes, she never condemned me. Rather, she taught me in a less abrasive way. During other times when I was distressed or worried, she used the power of humor to help heal my wounds.

My grandma knows just what to say in every situation. She is, to me, a wise woman, an orator using her stories like medicine.

As I got older and the problems of life seemed to intensify, my grandma handed me words of advice that I continue to use to this day. My husband, Steven, and my three month old daughter, Cyan, had just moved from California to Colorado. We were living in a hotel until we were able to close on our first house. We were supposed to stay in the hotel for only a week. I was not working and my husband had taken a new teaching job. A few days before we were supposed to take possession, we received a phone call that the house did not appraise. I was panic-stricken! We now had no house and were living in a hotel with our new baby. I spoke to my grandma, immediately, and she told me "from *Schlamazel comes Mazel.*" – or - from bad luck comes good luck. Sure enough in a few weeks, we were able to find and close on a different house in a different area. Last month, less than four year after all of this occurred, we were able to sell that house in eight days at full price. I truly believe had we not had the "*shlamazel*", we never would have received this "*mazel*"

Those words continue to ring true in my life. I know whenever something bad happens; something good will come from it. It is very reassuring!

My grandma, to me, is a magical woman. On the day of my wedding it was supposed to rain. Our ceremony was being held outdoors. My grandma assured us it wasn't going to rain during the ceremony. She had talked to her mother – long deceased - and it was taken care of. We had beautiful weather during our ceremony, from the time we arrived, until the last guest as well as my new husband and I got into our cars. As we drove away, a drop of rain fell upon our vehicle. Shortly after, it poured! Only my grandma could have pulled that off.

Introduction

Sarah (Sekie) Rothkopf is my father's first cousin. But, for as long as I can remember, I have called her Tante Seki. Tante is the Yiddish and French word for aunt. She always treated me as her niece -- certainly not as a distant cousin. So, from this point on, in this book Sarah (Sekie) Rothkopf will be referred to as "***My Tante.***"

Many people I've spoken to over the years can identify one person who has been instrumental in their development of ideas, values, etc. This is especially true of the successful people I've spoken to. Most research, in human development, supports the concept that having just one important and influential person, provides and strengthens resiliencies to withstand life's challenges In my life, this is ***My Tante***. Without particularly trying to or without having any ulterior motive, she has taught me lessons that stay with me in my everyday functioning, and especially in those times when I need to make important choices or decisions.

Not only have I lived and continue to live by much of what ***My Tante*** has taught me, I realize in my work, first as a counselor and now as a speaker, trainer, and coach, how often I refer to her teaching, quote her sayings and share her ideals.

It is for this reason that I have decided to write this book. It seems only logical that I continue to share her wonderful wisdom with the world. ***My Tante's*** messages are often simple and common sense. However, they seem to be of such things that people often miss or forget. Perhaps it's just the way she presents her messages that is special.

Please join me as I share with you the often humorous but so profound and enlightening ***Pearls From My Tante***.

Do You Know Your Hymmmms?

No matter how much we learn and how much we evolve, there are some things we just can't fully leave behind. It may be from our past, it may be cultural, or it may be habit. Or, it may be a combination of all these. We know how we're supposed to behave or we know what we're supposed to say, but there is this impulse just dying to jump out and take control. So, what to do?

My Tante taught me about *hymmmms*. See, when she found herself in the proverbial empty nest and decided to go back to school, she first took a psychology course. Remember, now, she came from a very traditional Brooklyn, Jewish family. If you know much about them, you'll know that boundaries are not a priority, if they exist at all. So, imagine the confusion when ***My Tante*** learned that it's not really OK to say to her married daughter "So, that's what you're serving for dinner – you couldn't make a real meal?"

This is when she learned her first hymn.-Her brain is telling her to be quiet; her daughter is married and living her own life now. But, those impulses from years of doing things differently are fighting hard. This is when she sits in a chair, holds onto the arms and *HYMMMM!*

Of course, ***My Tante*** is quick to point out that was the mother-in-law hymn. The grandmother hymn is much more difficult. That's when she wants to say "I'm cold, put a sweater on the baby." This creates a very loud *hymmmm*, so she goes into the closet.

I can't even imagine the *hymmmms* she's experiencing now as a great grandmother!

I've learned that the *hymmmms* don't have to be said out loud. I discovered this when my daughter, who had, creating much angst for me, decided to take time off college. I'd been the only one in my family to graduate college up to then. I was determined she would also. Despite my fears of her not going back, I had, for the most part, kept my mouth shut. I had to keep reminding myself this was not a crisis as she could always go back to school (see "*The Difference Between a Crisis and a Pain in My Tuchas*").

Anyway, one glorious day, my daughter came to our house to tell Keefe (my fiancé) and I that she was going back to school. She was saying all the things I'd said to her all her life. "Education is important if I'm going to have a good job." "I want to accomplish things and be able to have intelligent conversations, etc." Now, let me tell you, I wanted to scream, "I told you so!" But, I quietly said my *hymmmms.* In my head, I was saying "*hymmmm*" – a very long "*hymmmm.*" It's sometimes best to let others think their idea is original even when we know better.

Note:

Keefe and ***My Tante*** had much in common, particularly their sense of humor. This is probably why I love them both so much. When my darling, then, soon to be a college student, daughter left, my insightful and humorous fiancé came over and said “Let me massage your jaw, darling. I know the ‘I told you so’ is stuck and you are ready to choke on it.” That’s when I knew that my *hymmmm* worked, even if I kept it to myself. ***My Tante*** loved that one when I told her!

The Difference Between a Crisis and a Pain in the Tuchas

First, let me give you a bit of background information. I grew up in a home of crisis. I don't mean there were serious, honest to goodness crises. I mean, that a day was not complete without one. There seemed to be little difference between a crisis and an inconvenience. My mother thrived on crises and if she didn't have one, she'd join someone else's. Some crises were real, but exaggerated. Others just seemed to be imagined. Of course, I then learned that crises were attention getting and an important part of daily life. Looking back, I can't believe the big deal that was made out of fairly inconsequential events.

One day, when visiting ***My Tante,*** she asked me "Darling, do you know the difference between a crisis and a pain in the tuchas?"

Obviously, if she was asking, it was pretty clear that I didn't.

"Darling," she said again, "A crisis is life changing or life altering. Everything else is a pain in the tuchas. Don't get me wrong, sweetheart, there are big pains in the tuchas and there are little pains in the tuchas, but if it isn't life threatening or life altering, it isn't a crisis!"

Now this may seem like common sense. It certainly did when ***My Tante*** said it. But, how many people do you know -- maybe even yourself -- whose lives are fraught with "crises" that are really just pains in the tuchas? How many times do people put energy into something that can be handled with much less or maybe doesn't even need to be handled at all?

Don't get me wrong, some pains in the tuchas need to be taken care of or they could become a crisis. If you have a cold and it turns into bronchitis and then it turns into pneumonia because you refuse to go to a doctor, you could die. But having a cold is not a crisis; it is a real pain in the tuchas.

Most pains in the tuchas are time limited. I knew I was getting this concept when my washer and dryer decided to die within a week of each other. I was recently divorced and my credit was not what you'd call stellar. I went to Sears and worked with a very nice salesman who was trying to do what he could. Each time I went, we seemed to need one more thing. To make a long story short, I was in the store about four times in three days. At one point he said to me "Miss, you are very patient. Most customers would be screaming by now." To which I replied -- "This is a real pain in the butt (he might not have known what a tuchas was), but it's not a crisis. "It was a pain in the tuchas. I was taking my laundry to my friends. I was hanging things to dry everywhere in my house. But, I knew that eventually we would work things out and once we did, it would be no time before I forgot the inconvenience. And, even if we hadn't worked it out, many people go to Laundromats and none of them has ever died from it, as far as I know.

So, now when I find myself reacting to something, I stop for a moment and ask myself ***My Tante's*** question: "Is this a crisis or a pain in the tuchas?" Then, I take it from there. Whew! What a relief! So many less crises in my life!

Dirty Baby Sleeping

I don't know about you, but when my daughter was small, I tried to be the perfect parent – especially when someone else was looking. So, imagine if you will, how much I wanted to show ***My Tante*** what a perfect mom I was. I was soon to learn two things.

One: perfection is not necessary.

Two: perfection (or as close as we can come) often looks different than we think.

My daughter was an infant and we had just spent the day shopping, eating, and feeding the ducks at the duck pond. Needless to say, when we returned to ***My Tante's*** home, I had one rather grungy child. She was also a rather tired and cranky child. Wanting to be that perfect mom, I immediately began running bath water, while my child was whining, crying and very much in the need of a nap.

My Tante, in her usual wisdom and directness asked, "What ARE you doing?" To which I responded, "She's dirty." I thought it was pretty obvious.

My Tante: "She is dirty but she's more tired than dirty and I promise you she'll still be dirty when she wakes up – No baby ever died by taking a nap dirty - let her sleep!"

So, despite my discomfort and with the encouragement of one who is much wiser than I, we cleaned her face and her hands (we thought having a clean thumb to suck would be good) and put her to bed.

Guess what! She didn't die! I didn't die! And, the world didn't stop spinning on its axis! She was still dirty when she woke up, but she was happy! I was happy, and bath time was fun!

I learned the immediate lesson that day, but it took me quite some time to learn the larger lesson.

Let tired, cranky babies sleep!

Actually, there is more. Know what's important, but more importantly, know when it's most important. This has been applied to so many issues in my life.

The Meaning of Religion

Shared by Nicole Sneider Kaplan

My Tante's granddaughter Nicole shares another story. This one is of ***My Tante's*** views on the act of being religious.

> Great-grandma (GG) Sekie (***My Tante***) never pressured us to practice Judaism in a strict sense, by joining a temple or keeping kosher. Being religious to GG Sekie is being a good person. Her philosophy of being Jewish includes passing on family and community traditions, stories, lessons, cuisine and the Yiddish language of generations past. A good Jew is a good person, who opens their home, shares a meal, and lends a helping hand anytime. She taught us to welcome people into your home. A good Jew is not defined by membership in a synagogue or being kosher. We have learned from GG Sekie to live and let live, live with an open heart, acceptance, and empathy. But, have fun sharing traditions, family recipes, and stories and helping others. These values have helped shape our community of friends and family. Each holiday our home is full of folks to share in culinary traditions, to just be together, and to enjoy a Jewish family feast. It is always an extra special time when GG Sekie is able to join us.

This story touched me because it helped me recognize one of the reasons I've learned so much from ***My Tante.*** She doesn't push her views on others. She doesn't judge. She simply is! She lives her life in a way that is caring, open, and so accepting. When she speaks, it's hard not to listen because it's always said in the same loving manner.

I was welcomed into ***My Tante's*** home when I was a college student not far from her. She never nagged me. She never pushed. But I knew that the door was open and one phone call would get me in. When I was going through a divorce many years ago, her home was a haven. It was a place to be fed -- physically and spiritually. My Tante accepted, loved and without even knowing it, taught me. More recently, when I lost the love of my life, suddenly, without thought, I knew that ***My Tante*** was the one I needed to be with.

For me, ***My Tante's*** religion is not organized. It's spiritual. The spirit of being! The spirit of loving and accepting! The spirit of knowing that no one is perfect but deserves our love and acceptance! How much better my world is when I remember this one lesson from ***My Tante***.

Being Gentle

My Tante has a beautiful home with many collectables and wonderful objects. On my first visit to her home, after my daughter, Dania, had learned to walk, had me very concerned. Her house was not set up to easily block off areas with gates. ***My Tante's*** response was to not worry. But, worried, I was.

Upon arriving for our visit, I noted that nothing had been put away or placed up high. My anxiety was growing. But, leave it to ***My Tante.*** She had a plan.

As soon as my young daughter headed to the living room, ***My Tante*** followed. She picked up the first item my daughter showed interest in and let her touch it – with one finger. They then proceeded to explore the entire living room together – touching anything Dania wanted – with one finger.

When done with the exploration, Dania left the living room, willingly, with ***My Tante***. She showed little interest in all those pretty objects for the rest of our visit. When she did, all we needed to say was – "One Finger". Nothing was broken, no one was anxious and Dania was content. I was able to use this with Dania, no matter where we went.

Certainly, there's a great message for parents, grandparents - and Tantes, everywhere – in this story.

How many of us stifle the curiosity of children with the word, NO? How many of us are stifled, ourselves, out of fear or rejection - a different version of the word, NO?

My Tante's approach teaches us that we can experience all sorts of things. Sometimes, we need to wade in with care or we simply need to be gentle – with others or ourselves, exploring our world with "one finger" until we are able to grasp it with both hands.

So, go forth and touch!

The Power of Song

My Tante taught us all the power of song. My cousin Nicole (***My Tante's*** granddaughter) shares her story of how song helped her as a new parent.

I have witnessed this myself, both in years when my own daughter was young and more recently. She used song to sooth and direct toddlers long before Mary Poppins did with it with "a spoon full of sugar." She'd sing while giving a child a bath or while getting a defiant child dressed. She'd sing while teaching a child to play nice with a sibling or a cousin.

"GG (Great Grandmother) Sekie taught us the power of song over a defiant toddler. Any parent knows the frustration of managing a toddler and likely has accepted there is little control you have over certain behaviors. At the most frustrating times, GG Sekie breaks into song; songs that she has made up on the spot, but have stuck with the child and gently influence their behavior positively. Here are some examples, which you can sing to just about any tune."

Nicole Snieder Kaplan

Potty Training…

"Mommy and Poppy went to the potty, but Alex was quicker and she got a sticker."

Being patient…

"Let's be patient, let's be patient, some times we need to count to ten, 1, 2, 3, 4, 5, 6, 7, 8, 9, 10 Sometimes we need to count again, 1, 2, 3, 4, 5, 6, 7, 8, 9, 10

Slowing down (pull your arm up into your sleeve and walk slowly)…

> "The elephant carries his great big trunk, everywhere he goes. He has not lock and he has no key, so he carries it wherever he goes."

My own memories of ***My Tante*** are of her singing most of the time. When my own daughter was little, she would sign as they picked up toys. ***My Tante*** *would* sing while she fed her or helped her to bathe. The words didn't matter so much as the action of singing. Everything became fun and an adventure.

Now, I hear her singing to herself as she goes through her daily routine. ***My Tante*** has struggled with some physical difficulties that keep her from being as active as she might like. Instead of complaining she sings to herself.

> "I must bend down, I must keep moving. I may get there slowly but I'll get there eventually."

She even sings to my dog when I bring him to visit.

> "Gizmo needs to go out. Gizmo needs to go potty. Gizmo will get wet (if it's raining) but we'll get him dry before he knows it."

My Tante sings to herself, to children, to my dog, to anyone who may or may not be listening. She sings about what she's doing, what she's thinking, how she feels "creaky" when she moves, or how she forgets things. The message in this later act of singing is: life is what you make it. You can rail at the discomforts of life or you can deal with them -- with a smile and a song.

I've learned to use more song in our lives: to teach little children, to teach myself or just to entertain? I catch myself signing to my pets when I'm home alone. When I do this, I just smile and think of ***My Tante.*** I heard of a teacher in an inner city school, using RAP, to teach third graders math. She must have met ***My Tante.***

Trash Cans and Mallomars

My Tante taught me one of the most important but difficult lessons I've ever had to learn. She taught me that grief is not a neat and clean process of stages. While there are stages, as identified in much research, there is often little predictability to the emotions that go with these stages.

Shortly after her husband and love of many years, passed, I also lost the love of my life. My love had existed for a much shorter time but ***My Tante*** clearly let me know that it was no less a love or a loss than was hers – or anyone else's. Again, without saying so, in so many words, she shored me up and helped me to feel as normal as one can at such times.

A most lasting lesson was that we are human and logic has a way of leaving us just when we may need it most. Emotions have a way of popping up or dropping in when we least expect them. These emotions surprise us. The denial is not in place. We aren't prepared. We don't have our defenses up, and WHAM--There they are!

My Tante told me the story of the Mallomars (chocolate covered marshmallow cookies). My uncle apparently loved Mallomars. This was something my aunt couldn't eat, so she wouldn't buy them for herself, but every so often she'd buy them for my uncle Alvin. Well, there she was in the cookie aisle and there were the Mallomars. She instinctively reached for them and in an instant was overwhelmed. But this time, instead of a feeling of sadness she was angry. She was angry with him for dying. She was angry with him for not being there to buy Mallomars for. This didn't make sense; it doesn't have to. If I've learned one thing, it's that there is little sense to grief.

So, when I had my own irrational let down, I could only remember the Mallomars. Mine was a bit more humorous. Yes, there is humor, even in grief. ***My Tante*** taught me that, too. From the time Keefe moved in, I made it his job to take out the trash. I had never liked the job and was more than willing to give it up. I have a 90-foot driveway and especially in the winter, it was very nice to have someone else take over this odious job. When Keefe died in the month of December, I was immediately returned to trash duty. Several weeks later, I was taking the trash to the curb. There was snow and ice, and despite having a wheeled trashcan, I was struggling. I was also in my robe and had a pair of boots pulled on, as I'd forgotten about trash duty until after I was ready for bed. Well, about half way down the drive, I slipped. I fell on my tuchas. I wasn't hurt but I started crying. But, like my aunt, I wasn't sad. I was angry. I was cursing him, yelling, and carrying on. "It is not my job and why the hell aren't you here to do this?" I continued to do this for what felt like a long time. Thank goodness, my neighbors had their windows closed. I'm sure I used some fairly strong language. I never thought I could get that angry with Keefe. I didn't do this when he was alive. How could I be so angry with him now that he had died?

The next day, I sat and had a good laugh with a friend and recounted the Mallomars. I know that I could not have done this had ***My Tante*** not shared her story with me. I wonder, if in her wisdom, she knew, when she told me her story, that I'd need it in the near future.

It's Never Too Late!

It's important to remember that ***My Tante*** grew up in a different time and in a particular culture. She grew up in traditional Jewish Brooklyn. She lived the dream of the time: married, moving up (or out) to Long Island, and raising her daughters. For the most part, she didn't work outside the home. In fact, into in her 50s, she hadn't even had a reason to learn to drive. Though she had talked about it, and my Uncle Alvin had agreed to buy her a car if she learned, she was very intimidated by the idea of learning this new skill at this point in her life.

Flash forward several years! ***My Tante's*** daughters were out of the home. My uncle was working, and ***My Tante*** had fallen into a suburban routine. In addition to the daily chores of laundry, cleaning, and cooking (though, just for two now), there was a gathering at the local coffee shop with other women in the neighborhood.

My Tante may have fallen into an ordinary routine, but you must remember that *My Tante* is not an ordinary person. So, one day when one of the neighborhood ladies was recounting her day -- a very ordinary day where she described doing a few loads of dark and few loads of light -- a light went off in ***My Tante's*** head. Perhaps it was more like her brain exploding with boredom and intolerance for the mundane!

My Tante was raised to be a polite woman and she never lost sight of this, so she said nothing. But, as soon she returned home, she looked up the number and called a driving school. As she describes it, she was shaking and doubting herself. But, her absolute need to escape a life of repetition won! To hear her say it -- “Is this is all there is? White loads and dark loads? Teach me to drive and let me get out of here!”

So, ***My Tante*** learned to drive. She got her car and off she went to college! Life would never be the same. But, then if it had been, she wouldn’t be ***The Tante*** I know!

Most people can survive. Certainly, the other ladies in her neighborhood were doing a great job of surviving. However, life requires risk if you are to thrive. And if there’s one thing I’ve learned from ***My Tante*** it’s that life is about thriving rather than simply surviving!

As I go after my dreams, I will always remember, it’s never too late – nor, is it too early! I just need to get moving!

About The Author

Most importantly, Gayle is a mom, mother-in-law, grandmother, sister, friend and colleague; and of course, niece to Sarah (Sekie) Rothkopf – ***My Tante.***

Gayle has experienced many of the ups and downs in life including divorce, loss of her parents and the loss of a great love, as well as the every day events most face. Through these experiences, she has floundered, survived, and eventually learned to thrive.

As a result of her experiences, Gayle has created, **Living Lily** - Living Your Life Inspired by Living it Your Way! *(www.livingly.com)* Her philosophy is based on the concepts of making choices every day. Some are conscious, some not so. By exploring choices and making the best ones, we become the leaders in our own lives. Gayle's belief extends beyond everyday life, into business. Life, jobs, relationships and finances: all become choices, rather than chance.

While this may seem like common sense, it is often difficult to incorporate into daily thinking. This has lead to the creation of **LaSalle Consulting and Training** (www.lasalleconsultingandtraining.com), with a focus on corporate training where Gayle helps organization retain valued staff by teaching all to "play nice in the sandbox." The mission of **LaSalle Consulting & Training** is to help organizations retain their valued employees by increasing the morale and motivation needed for a productive workplace

Gayle LaSalle is a professional speaker and trainer with a message of hope, encouragement and need to lead life, in the best way possible. The development of LaSalle Consulting and Training and Living Lily combines these insights with Gayle's passion for education, training and helping people become all they can be.

Through speaking and training it is Gayle's goal, her mission, her pleasure to help others realize their ability to make choices and allow themselves to thrive rather than simply survive.

In addition to her formal training and personal experiences, Gayle credits many of her insights to Seki Rothkopf – ***My Tante***, her aunt, mentor and purveyor of wisdom. It is this wisdom and the role it plays in Gayle's life that has driven this book and Gayle's desire to share, with you, what has continually kept her somewhat sane or as sane as most of us can be.

If you have enjoyed this book or it has
touched you in some way,
I would love to hear from you
Please send any comments to:
Living Lily
151 Pashley Road
Glenville, NY 12302
Or e-mail – glasalle@nycap.rr.com

www.ingramcontent.com/pod-product-compliance
Ingram Content Group UK Ltd.
Pitfield, Milton Keynes, MK11 3LW, UK
UKHW041836200726
13854UKWH00003BA/1171

9 780557 06629